WILD
FLOWERS

A GUIDE TO   S
OF GREAT   E

JEAN RARAY

Translated by
J. G. BARTON

Photographs by
MARC BUZZINI

A LITTLE GUIDE IN COLOUR
PAUL HAMLYN · LONDON

Published by Paul Hamlyn Ltd
Drury House - Russell Street - London WC2
By arrangement with Golden Press, Inc.
© Copyright 1963 W.P.H.I., Genève
English translation © Copyright 1965 Paul Hamlyn Ltd
First published 1965
Second impression 1965
Printed in Italy by Arnoldo Mondadori Editore - Verona

CONTENTS

INTRODUCTION

Plants may be divided roughly into two groups; those that produce seeds, and those that do not. The latter, the cryptogams, include such plants as ferns, mosses, lichens, fungi and algae, and are not dealt with in this book. The plants that produce exposed seeds, the gymnosperms such as pines, larches and yews, are also excluded.

We are concerned here exclusively with the flowering plants or angiosperms, in which the seeds are completely enclosed within an ovary. This vast group forms the dominant vegetation over much of the earth's surface. It includes plants of endless variety of form and size, from tall forest trees to minute aquatics. A similar diversity is to be found in floral structure and, although we usually visualize flowers as being colourful, some, like those of the grasses, are green and inconspicuous. Some idea of this range can be gained by glancing through the illustrations on the following pages.

Well over two thousand species of flowering plants are found wild in Britain, but these represent only about two per cent of the known world flora. However, in spite of its relative paucity there is much of interest to be found in our native flora. Many are true 'natives', but whereas some are extremely common others are very rare and on the verge of extinction. In contrast, new species are always being brought into this country for agricultural and horticultural purposes. Some of these plants escape from cultivation and, if conditions are suitable, they spread so much that effectively they become new 'naturalized' members of our flora. Similarly, seeds are often brought in accidently with cargoes of various kinds, and these may give rise to 'casuals' which only persist for a short time.

Clearly the flora of Britain is not static but is constantly changing. Soil and climate affect the distribution of plants while in such a small densely-populated country man has also created a profound effect. Cultivation, afforestation, and the development of roads, railways and industry have greatly altered and will continue to alter the numbers and kinds of wild plants present in the countryside. Most of these activities have a deleterious effect on the vegetation, but in spite of them many species survive and some, when a suitable new habitat is created, tend to spread.

The coloured photographs show a selection of some of our common or interesting herbaceous plants and are representative of most of the larger families into which the angiosperms are divided. Each figure is accompanied by information about habitat, habit, season of flowering and fruit production. The scientific name of each plant and the family to which it belongs are also given. As a guide to the beginner there are sections on the naming and classification of plants at the end of the book, and the botanical terms used in the text are defined in the glossary.

THE FLOWERING PLANTS

THE LIFE SPAN Many flowering plants are trees or shrubs with persistent, woody stems but most of those illustrated in this book are herbaceous with soft, aerial stems which do not usually survive the winter. They can be separated into the following groups:

Annuals. In these the life-cycle is completed within a year. Generally the seed germinates in the spring and after a period of vegetative growth the flowers are formed. Following the production and release of the seeds the plant dies.

Biennials. These also flower once only but the life span covers two years. Vegetative growth occurs in the first year and the plant remains dormant during the winter. After renewed growth in the following year the plant flowers, fruits and then dies.

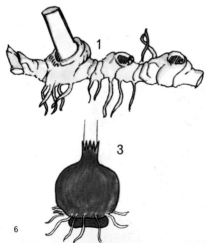

Perennials. These may live for a number of years and produce flowers repeatedly. All plants are securely anchored by an underground root system which absorbs water and nutrients from the soil, but perennial herbs also have some kind of swollen food-containing structure which allows them to persist during the winter. Generally all the parts above ground die each winter and new growth is produced from the underground perennating organ in the following spring. These structures may be:

1. *Rhizomes*, horizontal underground stems which can be short and thick (Solomon's Seal) or extensively creeping (Dog's Mercury);

2. *Bulbs*, short, erect stems with swollen scale leaves or leaf bases (Bluebell);

3. *Corms*, short, erect swollen stems covered with thin papery scales (Crocus);

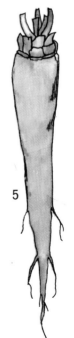

4. *Root tubers*, swollen roots which become detached from the parent plant (Lesser Celandine);

5. *Tap roots*, swollen main roots (Hawkbit).

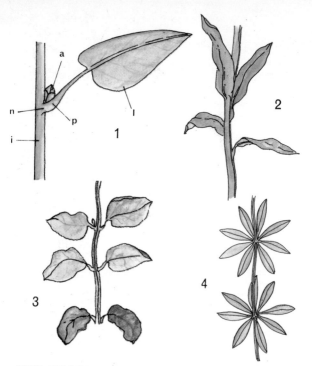

THE SHOOT SYSTEM The basic plan of the aerial shoot is shown in figure 1. The stem consists of elongated *internodes* (i) and *nodes* (n) to which the leaves are attached. The leaf has a blade or *lamina* (l) and a stalk or *petiole* (p). When a leaf has no stalk it is *sessile*. At the base of the leaf is an *axillary bud* (a) which may develop to form a branch.

The arrangement of leaves on the stem varies. As shown above they can be *alternate* (2, Forget-me-not), *opposite* (3, Creeping Jenny) or *whorled* (4, Sweet Woodruff).

TYPES OF LEAVES Leaves vary greatly in size and form. Some of the commoner leaf shapes are: 1, *linear* (Meadow Foxtail); 2, *lanceolate* (Lesser Periwinkle); 3, *ovate* (Bilberry); 4, *sagittate* (Arrowhead); 5, *trifoliate* (Clover); 6, *palmately compound* (Lupin); 7, *pinnately compound* (Valerian).

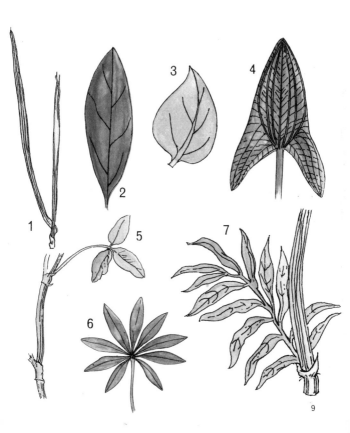

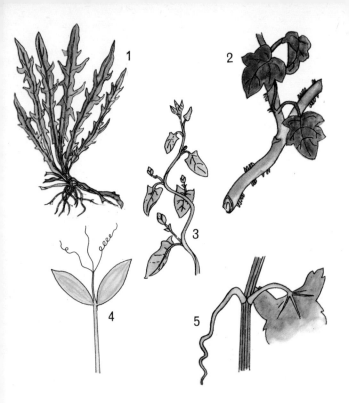

TYPES OF STEMS Many plants have stiff, erect self-supporting stems with long internodes. Others have a tufted habit with extremely short internodes and the leaves, which all arise at ground level, are described as *radical* (1, Hawkbit). Some plants have long, weak, climbing stems. These may become attached by special roots (2, Ivy) or actually twine around a support (3, Bindweed). Others have tendrils which may be modified leaflets (4, Meadow Vetchling) or stems (5, White Bryony).

TYPES OF INFLORESCENCES Flowers may be borne singly but more often they are grouped in inflorescences of various kinds. The flowers develop in sequence, the largest circle in each of the above diagrams representing the oldest one in the inflorescence. The main types are:

1, *spike* (Pondweed); 2, *raceme* (Willowherb); 3, *corymb* (Guelder Rose); 4, *umbel* (Ivy); 5, *capitulum* (Moon Daisy); 6, *cyme* (Ragged Robin).

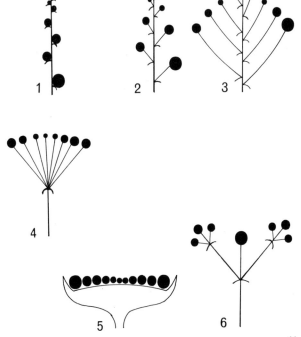

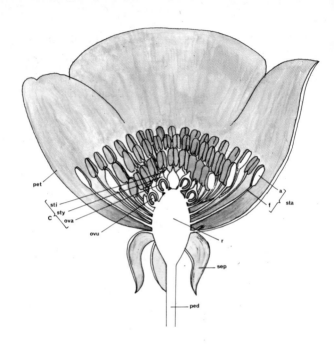

THE STRUCTURE OF FLOWERS Although flowers
vary greatly their basic structure can be seen in the
section of a Buttercup illustrated above. The flower
stalk or *pedicel* (ped) is terminated by the conicle *receptacle* (r). The outer whorl of *sepals* (sep) form the
calyx and above this is the *corolla* consisting of *petals*
(pet). Next comes the *androecium* of numerous *stamens*
(sta) each of which has a *filament* (f) and an *anther* (a)
containing the pollen grains. In the centre is the *gynoecium* of numerous *carpels* (c). Each carpel has an
ovary (ova) containing a single *ovule* (ovu), a short

style (sty), and a *stigma* (sti) on which the pollen germinates.

In contrast the flower of Honeysuckle has a very reduced calyx (ca) and a corolla (co) which is *sympetalous* (petals fused) and *zygomorphic* (bilaterally symmetrical). There are only five stamens (sta) and these are epipetalous, i.e. borne on the corolla. The gynoecium is *syncarpous* (with carpels fused together) and the ovary (ova) is *inferior*, i.e. below the other floral parts.

Each of the flowers shown here has both androecium

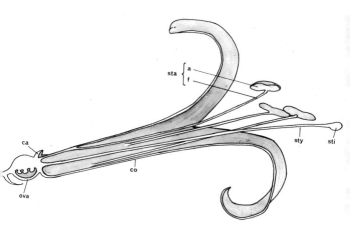

and gynoecium and is described as *hermaphrodite*. Some species have separate male and female flowers and these may be borne on separate plants (White Bryony).

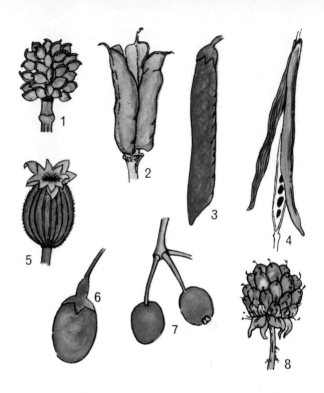

TYPES OF FRUITS The fruit develops from the ovary wall and contains the ripe seeds. It may be a group of separate one-seeded *achenes* (1, Buttercup) or of several *follicles* (2, Monkshood) which split open to release the numerous seeds. The *legume* (3, Meadow Vetchling), the *siliqua* (4, Wallflower) and the *capsule* (5, Ragged Robin) are also dry dehiscent fruits. A fleshy fruit may be a *berry* (6, Bittersweet), a *drupe* (7, Guelder Rose) or a group of *drupelets* (8, Blackberry).

GREAT REEDMACE *(Typha latifolia)*. This large perennial occurs in the shallow water of lakes and rivers. The thick rhizome growing in the mud bears erect linear leaves up to 8 feet long. The minute flowers are borne on stout stems during June and July. The male flowers are terminal and below these is a cylindrical mass of brown female flowers. The dry fruit opens to release the single seed **(Typhaceae).**

BUR-REED *(Sparganium ramosum)*. This grows in the shallow water of ditches and ponds. It has a perennial rhizome and erect leaves, triangular in section, up to 5 feet long. The small unisexual flowers are borne in globose heads on branched inflorescences produced between June and August. The heads of male flowers are borne above the female ones. Each fruit contains a single seed **(Sparganiaceae)**.

BROAD-LEAVED PONDWEED *(Potamogeton natans)*.
This is a common aquatic perennial of ponds and ditches.
It has an extensively creeping rhizome buried in the
mud. The submerged leaves are narrow but the floating
leaves have long stalks and ovate shiny blades, which
lie on the water surface. The short dense spikes of
small green flowers which project into the air are formed
between May and September **(Potamogetonaceae)**.

ARROW-HEAD *(Sagittaria sagittifolia)*, an aquatic plant found in the shallow water of ponds and canals. It roots in the mud and produces three types of leaves. The submerged leaves are strap-shaped, the floating leaves have heart-shaped blades which lie on the surface of the water and the aerial leaves have long stalks and erect sagittate blades. The branched aerial inflorescences, which appear in July or August, bear female flowers at the base and male flowers at the top. The fruit is a head of one-seeded achenes **(Alismataceae).**

WATER PLANTAIN *(Alisma plantago-aquatica)*. This is a herbaceous perennial which grows in the mud of shallow ponds and slow-flowing rivers. It varies from 6 inches to 3 feet in height. The large radical leaves have long stalks and ovate pointed blades which project above water surface. The flowers are produced on loose-branched panicles between June and August. Each flower has three green sepals, three thin white or pale pink petals and six stamens. The fruit consists of about twenty compressed one-seeded achenes **(Alismataceae)**.

FLOWERING RUSH (*Butomus umbellatus*). This attractive aquatic plant is occasionally found on the margins of ponds and canals. It is a perennial up to 4 feet in height with a rhizome buried in the mud and a rosette of long narrow leaves which projects above the water surface. The umbels of pink flowers are produced between July and September at the ends of stiff, unbranched stems. Each flower has three sepals, three petals and about nine stamens. The fruit consists of a group of follicles containing many small seeds **(Butomaceae)**.

COMMON QUAKING GRASS *(Briza media)*, also known as **Totter Grass,** is a perennial found mostly on chalky soils. It has a short rhizome and tufts of green leaves about 6 inches long. The loosely branched inflorescences which appear from June until August bear many small purplish pendulous spikelets. These are ovoid and each has four to twelve florets **(Gramineae).**

SWEET VERNAL GRASS *(Anthoxanthum odoratum)*
is a tufted perennial very common in meadows and
pastures. It has flat leaves and produces flowering
stems up to 18 inches high between April and June.
The compact inflorescence consists of many minute
one-flowered spikelets. This is a valuable pasture grass
which gives the characteristic smell to new-mown hay
(Gramineae).

MEADOW GRASS *(Poa pratensis)*. This is an extremely variable tufted perennial, commonly found as a constituent of grassland throughout the country. It has long, narrow, more or less flat leaves sheathing at the base. The erect stems, 6 to 30 inches high, appear from May until July and bear the spreading panicles. Each of the small flattened spikelets contains three to five florets **(Gramineae).**

BROME GRASSES *(Bromus* spp.*)*. These are annual or biennial grasses with loose inflorescences of fairly large spikelets. There are five to fifteen florets in each spikelet and these often have conspicuous awns. There are about eight species found wild in Britain. **Lop-grass** *(B. mollis)* is common in grassland and waste places. It is a very variable plant, 2 to 30 inches high, with compressed lanceolate spikelets. The other species illustrated here, **Field Brome** *(B. arvensis)*, is not a native but may be found occasionally. It has somewhat pendulous, long, narrow spikelets **(Gramineae).**

Field Brome   **Lop-grass**

COTTON GRASS *(Eriophorum angustifolium).* This perennial sometimes grows abundantly in wet bogs. It has long, creeping rhizomes and tufts of narrow leaves. The erect stems, 1 to 2 feet high, bear the small many-flowered spikes in May and June. The one-seeded fruits have long white hairs **(Cyperaceae).**

BULRUSH (*Schoenoplectus lacustris*) is a stout perennial forming large patches in lakes and rivers. It has a
creeping rhizome and erect leafless stems often 6 to
8 feet long. The cylindrical green stems are unbranched
and gradually taper towards the tip. The small flowers
are produced in June and July in brown ovoid spikelets
which form a dense inflorescence near the top of the
stem. The fruit is a small triangular nut containing a
single seed **(Cyperaceae).**

HERB PARIS *(Paris quadrifolia)*, is a perennial found occasionally on calcareous soils in damp woods. It has creeping underground rhizomes which give rise to straight unbranched stems about 15 inches high. Near the top of the stem are four (sometimes five) ovate pointed leaves. Between May and July a single stalked green flower is produced above them. The fruit is a fleshy black capsule containing the seeds. All parts of this plant are poisonous to man **(Trilliaceae).**

LILY-OF-THE-VALLEY *(Convallaria majalis)*. This perennial is a native plant frequent in woods on non-acid soils, but it has long been grown in gardens and often spreads outside them. It has a branched underground rhizome from which arise short, erect stems, each with two broad leaves about 9 inches long. The unbranched inflorescences, bearing six to twelve pendulous sweetly-scented flowers, appear in May and June. Each flower has a globular white perianth and six stamens. The fruit is a spherical red berry containing numerous seeds **(Liliaceae)**.

BUTCHER'S BROOM *(Ruscus aculeatus)*. This is a small, evergreen shrub found occasionally in dry woodlands. It has a creeping rhizome and stiff erect green stems up to 3 feet high. The ovate pointed structures which look like leaves are actually flattened stems (cladodes). The small greenish flowers appear between January and April in the axils of the tiny scale-like leaves on the surfaces of the cladodes. The male and female flowers are borne on separate plants. The fruit is a spherical red berry **(Liliaceae)**.

AUTUMN CROCUS *(Colchicum autumnale)* occurs sporadically in wet grassland. In late spring the underground corm produces several long narrow leaves. The single flowers appear from August to October. The perianth has six pale purple lobes and a long narrow tube with the ovary at the base. The fruit only emerges above ground in the following spring **(Liliaceae)**.

BLUEBELL *(Endymion non-scriptus)*. This well known woodland plant is especially common on somewhat acid soils. The soft white underground bulb produces a number of flat linear leaves early in the year while the racemes of four to fifteen flowers appear between April and June. Each flower has six blue perianth parts and six stamens. The fruit is an ovoid capsule containing numerous black seeds **(Liliaceae)**.

WILD DAFFODIL *(Narcissus pseudonarcissus)* is a true native in Britain and may be found in woods and grassland. The bulb produces a number of narrow leaves, followed by the solitary flowers between February and April. The perianth has six yellow spreading lobes and a long, narrow, deep-yellow trumpet or corona enclosing the six stamens. The inferior ovary forms a capsule containing numerous seeds **(Amaryllidaceae).**

PHEASANT'S EYE *(Narcissus poeticus)*. This is an extremely variable species and some forms have long been cultivated. One variety, *N. majalis*, has become naturalized in a number of places. The flowers, produced in May, have white spreading perianth lobes and a short yellow corona with a pale red margin. Many of our garden daffodils and narcissi are of hybrid origin involving several species **(Amaryllidaceae)**.

SNOWDROP *(Galanthus nivalis)*. Although often cultivated, the snowdrop is occasionally found wild in damp woods. It has a white underground bulb which gives rise between January and March to two narrow dark-green leaves and a single, stalked flower. The pendulous flower has six white perianth segments, six stamens with yellow anthers and a rounded ovary below the level of the perianth. The fruit is an ovoid capsule **(Amaryllidaceae)**.

Spotted Orchid

Bird's-nest Orchid

ORCHIDS *(Orchidaceae)*. This large family of perennial herbs is mostly tropical but there are over fifty species in Britain. Each flower has three sepals and one of the three petals often forms a large lobed lower lip (labellum). In most British species there is a single sessile anther with a mass of pollen in each sac. These pollen masses are transferred by insect visitors to the stimgatic surfaces of other flowers. After pollination the inferior ovary becomes a capsule containing many minute seeds.

Soldier Orchid

Late Spider Orchid   **Fly Orchid**

Spotted Orchid *(Dactylorchis maculata)* is fairly common in peaty habitats, **Bird's-nest Orchid** *(Neottia nidus-avis)* is a brown saprophyte of beechwoods and the **Soldier Orchid** *(Orchis militaris)* is a rare plant of grassy situations. The others illustrated here, **Late Spider Orchid** *(Ophrys fuciflora)*, **Fly Orchid** *(O. insectifera)* and **Early Spider Orchid** *(O. sphegodes)* are all uncommon chalk plants.

Early Spider Orchid

LESSER PERIWINKLE *(Vinca minor)*. This trailing evergreen shrub is found occasionally in woods and hedgerows. The rooting stems are up to 2 feet long and bear pairs of opposite, lanceolate, dark-green leaves. The stalked flowers are produced singly in the axils of the leaves from March until May. The blue corolla has five spreading lobes and a basal tube enclosing the five stamens and a central ovary. The fruit consists of two follicles containing few seeds, but they are rarely found in this country **(Apocynaceae)**.

BIRTHWORT *(Aristolochia clematitis).* Although not a native, this perennial herb has been cultivated for its medicinal properties and has become naturalized. It has a creeping rhizome, erect green stems up to 3 feet high, and heart-shaped leaves. The small axillary groups of pale-yellow flowers are formed from June until September. The fruit is a capsule **(Aristolochiaceae).**

SUN PLANT *(Portulaca grandiflora).* This is a native of Brazil which is often grown in gardens and sometimes grows wild. It is an annual about 6 inches high with cylindrical leaves and terminal groups of large flowers formed in June and July. The flowers may be yellow, red or purple and only open in direct sunlight **(Portulacaceae).**

RAGGED ROBIN *(Lychnis flos-cuculi)* is a perennial herb of marshes and wet fields. The stems are up to 2 feet high and have pairs of opposite, narrow leaves. The terminal groups of flowers appear in May and June. Each flower has five pink four-lobed petals. The fruit is a capsule which opens by five apical teeth **(Caryophyllaceae)**.

CHARTERHOUSE PINK *(Dianthus carthusianorum).*
This extremely variable Central European perennial is
often grown in gardens and occasionaliy grows wild.
It has stiff erect stems up to 18 inches high and opposite, narrow leaves. The scented deep-pink flowers appear in terminal groups from June to September. The
well known **Sweet William** *(D. barbatus)* is closely
related **(Caryophyllaceae).**

LESSER CELANDINE *(Ranunculus ficaria)*. This is common in woods and hedgerows, forming a dark-green carpet bearing many bright-yellow flowers in early spring. Each flower has three sepals and nine to fifteen elongated petals. By late summer all the aerial parts have disappeared, but the plant persists in the soil as small cylindrical root tubers which contain stored food material **(Ranunculaceae)**.

TRAVELLER'S JOY (*Clematis vitalba*) is a climbing plant which grows over trees and shrubs up to as much as 20 feet high. It is quite common on chalky and other non-acid soils. The young stems which bear the opposite, compound leaves are slender but the older ones are thick and woody. The white flowers, borne in loose cymes, have four sepals which are petal-like but are not true petals. In early autumn the heads of achenes are conspicuous owing to the silky plumes which they bear—hence the other common name **'Old Man's Beard'** **(Ranunculaceae)**.

PASQUE FLOWER *(Anemone pulsatilla)*. This beautiful plant is a perennial herb found occasionally in short grass on dry chalk soils. It has a basal rosette of pinnate hairy leaves. The solitary flowers are found in April and May on erect stems 5 to 12 inches long. Each has six purple perianth parts and many stamens. The fruit is a head of achenes bearing long silky plumes of hairs when mature **(Ranunculaceae)**.

ADONIS *(Adonis vernalis)*. This European plant is often grown in gardens. It is a perennial 6 to 12 inches high with crowded, very dissected leaves. The large terminal flowers are produced in March and April. Each has ten to fifteen narrow yellow petals and many stamens and carpels. The fruit is a head of achenes. **Pheasant's eye** *(A. annua)* which is an annual sometimes found as a weed on arable land, has small bright-red flowers **(Ranunculaceae)**.

GOLDILOCKS (*Ranunculus auricomus*) is a common woodland herb. It has a perennial rootstock and variable, lobed leaves. The erect few-flowered inflorescences, up to 18 inches high, are produced in April and May. Although some flowers may have five deep-yellow petals, most have fewer small ones or none at all. The fruit is a head of achenes **(Ranunculaceae).**

MONKSHOOD *(Aconitum napellus)* is a very variable species, one form of which, *A. anglicum*, is a native found occasionally in wet, shady places. There are also a number of cultivated varieties. It is a perennial herb with dissected leaves and erect stems 3 to 4 feet high. The mauve zygomorphic flowers are produced from May to July. The fruit consists of three follicles. All species of *Aconitum* are extremely poisonous **(Ranunculaceae)**.

WATER CROWFOOT *(Ranunculus peltatus)*. This is another variable aquatic plant common in shallow ponds and rivers. It has flexible branched stems, much dissected submerged leaves and lobed floating leaves. The white flowers which appear above the water between May and August have five sepals, usually five white petals and numerous stamens and carpels. The fruit is a head of achenes. There are a number of similar variable species in this country and they are often difficult to identify **(Ranunculaceae)**.

COLUMBINE *(Aquilegia vulgaris)* is a perennial herb
with dissected leaves, sometimes found in damp woods
on calcareous soils. The erect stems are up to 3 feet
high and bear the bluish pendulous flowers in May and
June. The five petals have long nectary spurs. The
fruit is a group of follicles containing numerous black
seeds **(Ranunculaceae).**

BRANCHING LARKSPUR *(Delphinium consolida).*
This is a European plant only occasionally found on
waste places and cultivated land. In nature it is an annual up to 18 inches high with bluish-purple flowers
produced in May and June. There are numerous biennial garden forms having flowers of various colours.
The fruit is a single follicle **(Ranunculaceae).**

FIELD NIGELLA *(Nigella arvensis)*. Although a common cornfield weed in Europe, this annual herb is only found occasionally in Britain. It has stems up to a foot long and dissected leaves. The flowers, which appear in June and July, have five pale-blue petaloid sepals. The fruit is a group of partially fused follicles **(Ranunculaceae)**.

STINKING HELLEBORE *(Helleborus foetidus)* is an uncommon perennial herb with an unpleasant smell. It grows in woods on calcareous soils and has green branched stems up to 2½ feet high and stalked, deeply-lobed leaves. The flowers are borne in terminal groups in March and April. Each flower has five green sepals with red margins, five to ten tubular nectaries and numerous stamens. The fruit is a group of follicles **(Ranunculaceae)**.

BARBERRY *(Berberis vulgaris)* has often been plant-
ed, and although it is sometimes found in hedgerows,
its status as a true native is questionable. It is a much
branched shrub up to 7 feet high with sharp trifid spines
and ovate toothed leaves. The pendulous groups of
globular yellow flowers appear in May and June. Each
flower has numerous perianth parts and stamens and
a central ovary. The fruit is an ovoid red berry **(Berberidaceae).**

FIELD POPPY *(Papaver rhoeas).* This is a common weed on cultivated land although its occurrence has been reduced by the use of chemical weed killers. It is a hairy annual herb up to 2 feet high with a branched stem and lobed leaves. The flowers are produced from June until August. Each has two sepals, four bright-red petals with black basal patches, and numerous black stamens. The fruit is a capsule with a ring of pores through which the many minute seeds are released **(Papaveraceae).**

COMMON FUMITORY *(Fumaria officinalis)*. This annual herb is a common weed on cultivated land. The pale-green stems are up to 2 feet high and have dissected leaves. The spikes of small pink flowers are produced from May until October. The flower is zygomorphic with the upper petal forming a hood over the three smaller ones. The six stamens are in two groups hidden by the corolla. The spherical green fruit contains a single seed **(Fumariaceae)**.

WALLFLOWER *(Cheiranthus cheiri)*. This familiar garden plant is a perennial herb which has become naturalized and is commonly found growing on walls. It has erect stems up to 2 feet high bearing many lanceolate leaves. The scented flowers are formed in a terminal raceme from April until June. Each flower has four sepals, four petals, six stamens and a central ovary. The fruit is a long narrow siliqua which opens from below upwards to release the pale-brown seeds **(Cruciferae)**.

LADY'S SMOCK *(Cardamine pratensis)* is a herbaceous perennial of wet grassy places. The annual erect stems are about a foot high. The leaves are pinnate, those of the basal rosette having rounded leaflets. The pale lilac (rarely white) flowers appear between April and June. The seeds are flung out when the long narrow fruits open suddenly **(Cruciferae).**

DYER'S ROCKET *(Reseda luteola).* This is a herbaceous biennial common on walls, cultivated land and waste places. It has erect stems 2 to 5 feet high and entire narrow leaves. The dense terminal racemes of greenish-yellow flowers appear between June and August. Each flower has four sepals, four petals and numerous stamens. The fruit is a capsule with three pores through which the minute dark-brown seeds are released **(Resedaceae).**

MEADOW SAXIFRAGE *(Saxifraga granulata)*. This small perennial herb is usually found in grassland on dry non-acid soils. It perennates during the winter by means of rounded bulbils. In spring these produce, at first, rosettes of leaves with lobed, kidney-shaped blades. The white flowers appear later, between April and June, in small groups on slender erect stems up to 15 inches high. The fruit is an ovoid capsule which contains many small seeds **(Saxifragaceae)**.

DOG ROSE *(Rosa canina).* This deciduous shrub, which is probably the most common wild rose in Britain, can be found in hedgerows and scrub. It has strong arching stems covered with curved prickles. The pinnate leaves have two to three pairs of ovate serrate leaflets. The flowers are formed in small groups in June and July. Each has five green sepals, five large white or pink petals and numerous stamens. The ovoid fruit or hip is red when ripe and contains numerous separate achenes. Many varieties of this species have been described **(Rosaceae).**

BRAMBLES *(Rubus* spp.)*. These deciduous shrubs are common in hedgerows and woods. They have stout, prickly, biennial stems and alternate compound leaves. The white or pink flowers have five petals and numerous stamens. The red or black fruit is a group of fleshy drupelets. The extremely variable Blackberry *(R. fruticosus)* has been separated into many species **(Rosaceae).**

WILD STRAWBERRY *(Fragaria vesca)*. This perennial herb, which spreads by long rooting runners, is common in hedges and woods on non-acid soils. Each leaf has a long stalk and three serrated leaflets. The small white flowers are formed from April to July on stems about a foot high. After development the one-seeded achenes remain attached to the swollen red receptacle, thus forming a 'false' fruit **(Rosaceae)**.

LUPINS *(Lupinus* spp.*)*. Most of the three hundred known species of Lupins are American. They may be annuals or perennials with large palmate leaves. There are no native species in Britain, but some are cultivated and of these the **Tree Lupin** *(L. arboreus)* and **Perennial Lupin** *(L. polyphyllus)* may now grow wild. The one illustrated *(L. albus)*, is a Mediterranean annual used to improve poor soils **(Papilionaceae)**.

COMMON MELILOT *(Melilotus officinalis)*. This is a naturalized plant, sometimes common on waste ground. It is an erect branched perennial about 3 feet high with stalked, trifoliate leaves. The dense spikes of yellow flowers are formed between July and September. The calyx is five-toothed and the zygomorphic corolla is typical of the Pea family. The fruit is a short flattened pod which contains a single seed. Melilot has been used as a pot-herb and in medicine **(Papilionaceae)**.

1

2

CLOVERS (*Trifolium* spp.). About twenty different clovers occur wild in Britain, of which several are very common. They are annual or perennial herbs with trifoliate leaves and dense heads of small flowers. Both calyx and corolla persist round the fruit, which is a small pod containing one or a few seeds. The species illustrated here are: 1. **Crimson Clover** (*T. incarnatum*) a Mediterranean plant often cultivated and naturalised; 2. **Red Clover** (*T. pratense*) a native plant grown for hay; 3. **White Clover** (*T. repens*) also a common native species **(Papilionaceae)**.

3

BIRDSFOOT *(Ornithopus perpusillus)* is a small, prostrate hairy annual common on dry siliceous soils. The slender spreading stems of up to 18 inches long have pinnate leaves with five to twelve pairs of narrow leaflets. The minute whitish-yellow flowers are produced in small groups between May and August. The fruits are slender, curved, divergent pods and give the appearance of a bird's foot. The pods are constricted and break up into one-seeded portions **(Papilionaceae)**.

Everlasting Pea

PEAS (*Lathyrus* spp.). There are several common wild species of this genus in Britain. They are mostly herbaceous annuals or perennials with long angled stems, pinnate leaves, and tendrils by means of which they climb. The **Everlasting Pea** (*L. latifolius*), a South European plant with rose-pink flowers, has become naturalized in a few places. **Meadow vetchling** (*L. pratensis*), with yellow flowers produced between May and August, is common in meadows and pastures **(Papilionaceae).**

Meadow Vetchling

COMMON STORKSBILL *(Erodium cicutarium)*. This is a herb up to 18 inches high with variable, dissected leaves. It is commonest near the sea. The pinkish-purple flowers, formed between May and September, are borne in small groups at the end of thin stalks. Five of the ten stamens are sterile. The fruit consists of five one-seeded compartments at the base of a long beak-like projection **(Geraniaceae)**.

WOOD SORREL *(Oxalis acetosella)* is a small perennial often abundant in damp shady woods. It has a slender creeping rhizome which gives rise to the long-stalked trifoliate leaves. The persistent leaf bases are swollen with food reserves. The flowers are solitary and appear in April and May. Each has five pale petals with mauve veining. The fruit is a capsule from which the seeds are violently ejected **(Oxalidaceae)**.

DOG'S MERCURY *(Mercuralis perennis)* is a perennial herb common in shady woods. It has slender underground rhizomes and annual stems 8 to 18 inches high. The opposite, toothed leaves are dark-green. The flowers are unisexual and borne on separate plants. The fruit is a capsule which opens by two valves to release the two seeds **(Euphorbiaceae)**.

Sun Spurge

SPURGES *(Euphorbia* spp.*)*. The seventeen species found wild in Britain are all small herbs possessing a milky juice. The inflorescence bears a number of cup-like structures each enclosing a central stalked female flower and several male flowers. The fruit is a capsule containing three seeds. **Sun Spurge** *(E. helioscopia)* is a common annual weed, 4 to 24 inches high, with ovate leaves. **Cypress Spurge** *(E. cyparissias)* is a rhizomatous perennial with linear leaves and yellow inflorescences **(Euphorbiaceae)**.

Cypress Spurge

ALDER BUCKTHORN *(Frangula alnus)*. This is a deciduous tree or shrub up to 16 feet high which is common in suitable wet, peaty habitats. The alternate leaves have ovate, pointed blades. The groups of small flowers are borne in the axils of the leaves on young twigs during May and June. The ovary, at first green, becomes red and finally black as it develops into the fleshy fruit containing about two seeds **(Rhamnaceae).**

COMMON MALLOW *(Malva sylvestris)*. This is a hairy, herbaceous perennial commonly found on roadsides and waste places. The erect stems are up to 3 feet high and bear alternate leaves with long stalks and round, lobed blades. The conspicuous rose-lilac flowers appear in clusters in the axils of the leaves between June and September. The fruit consists of one-seeded portions which separate at maturity **(Malvaceae).**

COMMON ROCKROSE *(Helianthemum chamaecistus)* is found on non-acid grassland. It is a perennial shrub about a foot high with thin, woody stems and opposite, ovate leaves. The yellow flowers, which are produced from June to September, have five petals and numerous stamens. The fruit is an ovoid capsule **(Cistaceae).**

SWEET VIOLET *(Viola odorata)* is common in hedgerows and scrub on calcareous soils. It is a small perennial herb with a rhizome and heart-shaped leaves. The scented purple flowers, found singly on long stalks between February and April, are pollinated by bees. Later, small flower buds are formed which produce viable seed although they do not open. The fruit is a round capsule **(Violaceae).**

PURPLE LOOSESTRIFE *(Lythrum salicaria)* is a perennial herb commonly found on the banks of ponds and rivers. It has erect stems about 3 feet high and opposite, lanceolate leaves. The attractive spikes of reddish flowers appear between July and September. Each flower has a tubular calyx, six petals and twelve stamens. The fruit is an ovoid capsule containing numerous small seeds **(Lythraceae)**.

EVENING PRIMROSE *(Oenothera biennis)*. This North American plant has become naturalized on waste places and railway banks. It is a stout hairy biennial with lanceolate leaves and erect stems up to 4 feet high. The large yellow flowers, which are formed from June to September, open in the evening and are strongly scented. The fruit is a capsule opening by four valves to release the minute seeds **(Onagraceae).**

ROSEBAY WILLOW-HERB *(Chamaenerion angusti-folium)*. This is a perennial, common on waste ground and woodland clearings. It has a spreading underground rhizome and erect stems up to 4 feet high with narrow pointed leaves. The flowers, formed from July until September, have four sepals, four pink petals and eight stamens. The fruit is a long narrow capsule **(Onagraceae)**.

IVY *(Hedera helix)*. This woody climber becomes attached to its support by special roots. It is common on walls and trees and also on the ground in shady woods. The leaves are often deeply lobed, but on the flowering stems they are simple. The dense umbels of greenish-yellow flowers appear between September and November. The fruit is a black berry with few seeds **(Araliaceae)**.

FIELD ERYNGO *(Eryngium campestre)*. This is a rare perennial found in a few places, usually on dry chalk soils. It is 1 to 2 feet high with branched stems and spiny leaves. The small white or purplish flowers are borne in dense ovoid heads in July and August. Another species, the **Sea Holly** *(E. maritimum)* is a somewhat coarser plant which is common on sandy shores **(Umbelliferae)**.

WILD CARROT *(Daucus carota)*. This is a biennial herb common in waste places especially near the sea. It has rigid erect stems 1 to 3 feet high and dissected leaves. The umbels of many small white flowers are formed between June and August. The fruit breaks up into two one-seeded portions covered with spines **(Umbelliferae)**.

FOOL'S PARSLEY *(Aethusa cynapium)* is an annual weed, 2 inches to 4 feet in height, with very divided leaves. The flowers, similar to those of the **Wild Carrot,** appear in July and August **(Umbelliferae)**.

81

COW PARSLEY *(Anthriscus sylvestris)* is an extremely common hedgerow perennial. It has thick erect stems up to 4 feet high and large, greatly dissected leaves. The compound umbels of white flowers appear from April to June. The calyx is represented by five minute teeth. The five petals are often unequal in size in the marginal flowers of the umbel. The inferior ovary develops into a fruit consisting of two one-seeded parts **(Umbelliferae).**

BILBERRY *(Vaccinium myrtillus)*, also known as **Whortleberry** or **Whimberry,** is common in heaths and moors on siliceous soils. It is a deciduous shrub with spreading underground rhizomes. It has erect green stems bearing simple oval leaves. The solitary pendulous flowers, which appear between April and June, have pinkish-green globular corollas. The fruits are round blueblack berries which are often collected and used for making jams and pies **(Ericaceae).**

LING *(Calluna vulgaris)*. This is very common on the acid soils of heaths and moors. It is an evergreen shrub with wiry stems up to 3 feet high and small, dark green, four-ranked leaves. The flowers, which have both calyx and corolla of the same rose-purple colour, are borne in dense terminal spikes between July and September **(Ericaceae)**.

CROSS-LEAVED HEATHER *(Erica tetralix)* is a common woody evergreen perennial in the wetter parts of moors and heaths. The small leaves are in whorls of four. The flowers, which appear on the upper parts of the stem from July to September, each have a small green calyx and a pink ovoid corolla. The capsule contains many seeds **(Ericaceae).**

COWSLIP *(Primula veris)* is often abundant in grassy places on calcareous soils. It is a hairy perennial herb with a short rhizome and ovate, crinkled, radical leaves. The erect stems, 4 to 12 inches long and bearing up to thirty terminal flowers, appear in April and May. Each flower has an inflated calyx, a yellow corolla with five spreading lobes, five epipetalous stamens and a central ovary. The fruit is an ovoid capsule. **Primrose** *(P. vulgaris)* has larger flowers but where this grows with the **Cowslip,** intermediate hybrids between the two are found **(Primulaceae).**

YELLOW LOOSESTRIFE *(Lysimachia vulgaris)* is a perennial herb found beside ponds and rivers. It has a rhizome and erect stems 2 to 5 feet high. The lanceolate leaves are in whorls of three or four. The terminal inflorescences of yellow flowers appear in July and August. The fruit is a globose capsule which opens by five valves to release the numerous seeds **(Primulaceae).**

SCARLET PIMPERNEL *(Anagallis arvensis)*. This is an annual herb commonly found on disturbed ground, sand dunes and as a weed of cultivated land. It has weak branched stems up to a foot long and pairs of opposite, ovate leaves. The flowers are produced singly, on long stalks in the leaf axils, from May to September. The shallow corolla has five lobes and is usually red, although occasionally it may be pink or blue. The fruit is a small spherical capsule which opens by means of a lid **(Primulaceae)**.

JERSEY THRIFT *(Armeria arenaria)*. This perennial, which occurs on sand dunes in Jersey, is somewhat larger than our common **Sea Pink** *(A. maritima)*. The latter is common on salt-marshes, rocks and cliffs by the sea. The plant is tufted with many narrow, dark-green leaves. The heads of pink or white flowers are formed between April and October **(Plumbaginaceae).**

GENTIAN *(Gentiana asclepiadea).* This is an alpine plant found mostly on limestone rocks and it does not occur in Britain. It is a perennial 1 to 3 feet high with lanceolate leaves. The handsome flowers, which are borne in small axillary groups from July to September, each have a blue trumpet-like corolla and five epipetalous stamens. The fruit is a capsule containing numerous small seeds. There are eight wild Gentians in Britain but only **Felwort** *(Gentianella amarella)* and **Field Gentian** *(G. campestris)* are at all common **(Gentianaceae).**

BOGBEAN *(Menyanthes trifoliata)*. This is an aquatic perennial common in shallow ponds and wet bogs. It has a creeping rhizome and large aerial trifoliate leaves. The spikes of attractive flowers appear between May and July. The corolla is white or slightly pink and has long hairs on its inner surface. The fruit is a capsule opening by two valves **(Menyanthaceae).**

LARGE DODDER *(Cuscuta europaea)* is a rare parasite found mostly on Stinging Nettles. Soon after seed germination it loses all contact with the ground. The reddish stems twine around the host, from which they absorb water and nutrients. The groups of small flowers are formed in August and September. The fruit is a capsule containing two seeds **(Convolvulaceae).**

BINDWEED *(Convolvulus arvensis)* is common in waste places and as a weed of cultivated land. Owing to its deep-growing, brittle rhizomes it is a difficult plant to eradicate. The weak climbing stems twine round any support they can reach in an anticlockwise direction. The leaf blades are sagittate. The flowers are borne in small groups, in the axils of the leaves, from June to September. The flower is about an inch across with a funnel-shaped, white or pink corolla. The fruit is an ovoid capsule containing few seeds **(Convolvulaceae).**

VIPER'S BUGLOSS *(Echium vulgare)* is a biennial found in dry, grassy places. It has a tap root, a rosette of lanceolate leaves and erect stems up to 3 feet high. The flowers, all facing in one direction, appear from June until September. The blue corolla is funnel-shaped and four of the five stamens project beyond it. The fruit consists of four one-seeded nutlets **(Boraginaceae).**

FORGET-ME-NOTS *(Myosotis* spp.*)*. These are small hairy annual or perennial herbs with alternate lanceolate leaves. The blue flowers are borne in terminal scorpoid cymes. The corolla is pink at first but as the flower opens it becomes blue. The fruit consists of four nutlets surrounded by the persistent calyx. There are ten

Water Forget-me-not

Wood Forget-me-not

native species in Britain. One of the **Water Forget-me-nots** *(M. scorpioides)*, is common by streams and ponds and the **Wood Forget-me-not** *(M. sylvatica)* occurs in moist woods **(Boraginaceae).**

RED DEAD-NETTLE *(Lamium purpureum)*. This is a very common annual herb in waste and cultivated land. It is 6 to 18 inches high and the square stems bear pairs of opposite, ovate leaves. The flowers, which appear between March and November, have a calyx with five teeth and a reddish corolla. The fruit consists of four small nutlets **(Labiatae)**.

GIPSYWORT *(Lycopus europaeus)* is a common perennial on the sides of ponds and rivers. It has a rhizome, erect stems 1 to 3 feet high, and pairs of opposite, lobed leaves. The small white flowers, which have only two stamens, are produced in compact groups in the axils of the upper leaves from June until September **(Labiatae).**

MINTS *(Mentha spp.)*. There are about seven wild species of mints in Britain but as they are extremely variable, and hybridize freely, identification is often difficult. They are scented perennial herbs with creeping rhizomes and pairs of opposite leaves. The flowers, borne in loose or dense axillary whorls, may be purple, white or pink. Each flower has a tubular, toothed calyx, a four-lobed zygomorphic corolla and four epipetalous stamens. The fruit consists of four one-seeded nutlets. Among our commoner species are **Corn Mint** *(M. arvensis)*, **Water Mint** *(M. aquatica)* and **Apple-scented Mint** *(M. rotundifolia)*. The cultivated **Spearmint** *(M. spicata)* has often become established in waste places **(Labiatae)**.

WILD MARJORAM *(Origanum vulgare)* is a common perennial in dry grassy places on calcareous soils. The erect stems are 1 to 2 feet high with the small rose-coloured flowers borne in dense terminal inflorescences. The calyx has five teeth and the corolla is two-lipped. The four stamens are borne on the corolla and usually project beyond it. Marjoram is aromatic and often used as a pot-herb **(Labiatae)**.

HEDGE WOUNDWORT *(Stachys sylvatica)* is common in damp shady woods and hedges. It has a perennial rhizome and erect stems up to 3 feet high which bear pairs of opposite leaves with heart-shaped blades. The flowers are borne on terminal spikes between July and September. The reddish-purple corolla has a hooded upper lip concealing the four stamens and a three-lobed, mottled lower lip **(Labiatae)**.

WILD THYME *(Thymus serpyllum)* is an extremely variable perennial common on dry heaths and grassland. It forms a dense carpet, about 3 inches high, of thin stems with small ovate leaves. The terminal heads of tiny pinkish flowers are formed in July and August. Each flower has a two-lipped corolla and four projecting stamens. The fruit consists of four one-seeded nutlets **(Labiatae).**

BUGLE *(Ajuga reptans)* is a small perennial herb common in damp shady places. It has a rhizome and also spreads by creeping stolons. The erect stems, 4 to 12 inches high, bear pairs of ovate leaves. The elongated inflorescences are formed between June and September. The blue corolla has a very small upper lip beyond which the four stamens project **(Labiatae).**

THORN-APPLE *(Datura stramonium)*. This is not a native plant but it has become established in a few places. It is a stout herb about 3 feet high with large ovate coarsely-toothed leaves. The flowers occur singly in the axils of the upper leaves from July to October. The calyx is pale-green and the long narrow corolla is white or purple. The fruit, often covered with large spines, is a large ovoid capsule which opens by four valves to release the many seeds. All parts of this plant are highly poisonous **(Solanaceae).**

HENBANE *(Hyocyamus niger)* is a biennial herb found on waste ground, especially in sandy soil near the sea. The erect hairy stems about 2 feet high have alternate lobed leaves. The flowers, formed between June and August, have cream-coloured, lobed corollas marked with purple veins. The fruit is a capsule which opens by a lid to release the numerous small seeds **(Solanaceae).**

BITTERSWEET *(Solanum dulcamara)* occurs in hedgerows and woodland margins. It is a perennial with long woody scrambling stems and alternate, lobed leaves. The flowers appear in small groups between June and September. The corolla has five purple lobes and the large yellow anthers of the five stamens form a conspicuous cone around the ovary. The fruit is a red berry **(Solanaceae)**.

DEADLY NIGHTSHADE *(Atropa bella-donna)* is a rare herbaceous perennial occuring in hedgerows or near buildings on calcareous soils. The stems are up to 5 feet high and have ovate, pointed leaves. The axillary flowers are borne on long stalks, singly or in pairs, from August until October. The greenish-violet, bell-shaped corolla is about an inch long and has five obtuse lobes. The fruit is a shiny black berry containing many seeds. All parts of this plant are extremely poisonous **(Solanaceae).**

AARON'S ROD (*Verbascum thapsus*). This is a biennial found in dry open situations. The erect stems are 1 to 6 feet high and bear broad lanceolate leaves, the basal ones being up to 18 inches long. The whole plant is covered with white woolly hairs. The yellow flowers, which are produced on dense terminal spikes between June and August, have a shallow five-lobed corolla and five stamens. The fruit is an ovoid capsule containing many small seeds **(Scrophulariaceae)**.

FIGWORT *(Scrophularia nodosa)*. This perennial herb is common in wet hedgerows and woods. It has a tuberous rhizome, erect angled stems up to 3 feet high, and opposite, ovate leaves. The loose terminal inflorescence is formed between July and September. Each small flower has a short five-toothed calyx, a tubular two-lipped greenish-brown corolla and four epipetalous stamens. The fruit is an ovoid capsule which opens by two halves **(Scrophulariaceae)**.

FOXGLOVE *(Digitalis purpurea)* is a biennial which is often to be found in hedgerows and woodland clearings, especially on dry acid soils. It has a rosette of large, ovate leaves and an erect stem up to 3 feet high which terminates in the long inflorescence between May and September. The tubular corolla is usually purplish-pink or occasionally white. The fruit is an erect ovoid capsule containing many small seeds **(Scrophulariaceae).**

Brooklime

SPEEDWELLS *(Veronica* spp.). There are over twenty species in Britain. They are annual or perennial herbs with opposite leaves and small blue flowers. The fruit is a capsule. **Brooklime** occurs in very wet situations and **Germander Speedwell** in hedgerows and cultivated ground **(Scrophulariaceae).**

Germander
Speedwell

WEASEL'S SNOUT *(Antirrhinum orontium)* is an annual found occasionally as a weed of cultivation. The erect stems are 8 to 20 inches high and bear linear leaves. The axillary pink flowers, produced between July and October, are similar in structure to those of the well known **Snapdragon** *(A. majus)*, but are much smaller. The fruit is a capsule **(Scrophulariaceae).**

TOADFLAX *(Linaria* spp.*)*, ·are herbs with simple narrow leaves. The flowers are similar to those of *Antirrhinum*, but the corolla has a long spur. The fruit is a capsule. The most frequent of the several wild British species is the **Common Toadflax** *(L. vulgaris)*, which occurs in grassy places. The racemes of yellow flowers are formed from July to October. *L. petraea* is a small alpine plant **(Scrophulariaceae).**

Common Toadflax

Linaria petraea

BROOMRAPES (*Orobanche* spp.). There are eleven wild species of these interesting parasitic herbs in Britain. They are annual or perennial and become attached to the roots of their hosts by tubers. They are non-green and rely entirely on their host plants for nutriment. The erect brown flowering shoots, 6 to 30 inches high, appear above ground between May and September. The flower has a two-lipped corolla and four stamens. The fruit is a capsule containing many minute seeds **(Orobanchaceae).**

Cleavers

BEDSTRAWS *(Galium* spp.*)*. These are slender annual or perennial herbs with whorls of simple leaves and minute crowded flowers. There are about fifteen species in Britain and several are common. **Cleavers** *(G. aparine)* climbs over hedgerow plants aided by stiff, curved hairs while **Lady's Bedstraw** *(G. verum)*, common in grassland, has dark green leaves and yellow flowers **(Rubiaceae)**.

Lady's Bedstraw

WILD MADDER *(Rubia peregrina)* is a perennial ever-green occasionally found in hedgerows in Southern England. It has long, scrambling, sharply-angled stems and whorls of ovate, dark-green, leathery leaves with prickly edges. The groups of small yellow-green flowers are produced from June until August. The fleshy sphe-rical black fruit contains a single seed **(Rubiaceae).**

ELDER *(Sambucus nigra)*. This is a shrub or sometimes a small tree which grows up to 30 feet high. It is very common in waste places, woodland and scrub. The stout, much-branched stems are covered with a grey bark and bear pairs of opposite pinnate leaves with five to seven ovate leaflets. The large flat-topped inflorescences of many small creamy-white flowers are produced in August and September. Each flower has a minute calyx, a saucer-shaped corolla with five lobes and five stamens. The fruit is a black ovoid fleshy drupe containing few flattened seeds **(Caprifoliaceae)**.

HONEYSUCKLE *(Lonicera periclymenum)* is common in woods, hedgerows and among rocks. It is a twining shrub which often trails along the ground but may grow up to 15 feet high. The pairs of opposite, ovate leaves are dark-green. The terminal groups of scented flowers appear in June and September. Each flower has a calyx of five small teeth, a deep-cream tubular corolla ending in two reflexed lips, and five projecting epipetalous stamens. After pollination, by bumble bees or hawk moths, the inferior ovary becomes a round red berry containing a few seeds **(Caprifoliaceae).**

GUELDER ROSE *(Viburnum opulus)*. This deciduous shrub, which grows up to 15 feet high, is common in hedgerows especially on wet soils. The leaves, borne in opposite pairs, have long stalks and lobed blades. The white flowers appear in June and July in large flat inflorescences. The marginal flowers are sterile and much larger than the inner fertile ones. The fruit is an ovoid red drupe containing a single seed. There is a cultivated variety known as the **Snowball Tree** (var. *roseum*). This, as shown in the illustration, has only large sterile flowers and does not produce any seed. The **Wayfaring Tree** *(V. lantana)* is a common shrub on calcareous soils **(Caprifoliaceae)**.

VALERIAN *(Valeriana officinalis)*. This is a perennial herb commonly found in wet marshy ground although it also occurs in dry grassy situations. It has erect stems 1 to 5 feet high and compound pinnate leaves. The small, pale-pink flowers are produced in dense terminal inflorescences between June and August. The calyx consists of many inrolled teeth on the upper edge of the inferior ovary. The corolla has a short tube and five somewhat unequal lobes. The three projecting stamens are attached to the corolla tube. The fruit contains a single seed and possesses a crown of pappus hairs which develop from the calyx after fertilization **(Valerianaceae)**.

FIELD SCABIOUS *(Knautia arvensis)*. This is a variable perennial herb of dry grassland. It has a stout tap root, a basal rosette of lanceolate leaves and erect hairy stems 1 to 3 feet high. The capitula, which are formed between July and September, consist of numerous flowers, the marginal ones being longer than the rest. Each mauve flower has a toothed calyx, a corolla tube with four unequal lobes, four epipetalous stamens and an inferior ovary. The fruit contains a single seed **(Dipsacaceae)**.

TEASEL *(Dipsacus fullonum)*. This is a biennial herb sometimes found in waste places, particularly on clay soils. It has lanceolate leaves and stout prickly stems up to 6 feet high. The large stalked cylindrical heads of reddish-purple flowers appear in July and August. Intermingled with the flowers are sharply-pointed projecting bracts which, in **Wild Teasel** (ssp. *fullonum*), are straight and weak. However, in **Fuller's Teasel** (ssp. *sativus*), the bracts are stiff and curved and the dried heads are used for raising the nap on cloth **(Dipsacaceae).**

WHITE BRYONY *(Bryonia dioica).* This is a perennial herb, fairly common in hedgerows and scrub. It has a large underground tuberous rootstock which produces long green hairy stems. These scramble over other plants and become attached to them by spirally coiled tendrils. The alternate, stalked leaves have palmately-lobed blades. The yellowish-green flowers, which appear between May and September, are unisexual. The male flowers have five stamens with yellow anthers while the female flowers, which are borne on different plants, each have a central green ovary. The fruit is a red or orange berry containing a few flat seeds **(Cucurbitaceae).**

CAMPANULAS *(Campanula* spp.*)*. These are biennial or perennial herbs. The flowers are usually blue or purple and the corolla is more or less bell-shaped. There are five free stamens and the ovary develops into a capsule containing many seeds. There are about eleven species found wild in Britain. **Clustered Bellflower** *(C. glomerata)* is a perennial sometimes found on chalk grassland. The conspicuous bluish-purple flowers are produced from May until September. **Rampion** *(C. rapunculus)*

is an introduced biennial found only rarely, on siliceous soils. The common **Harebell** is *C. rotundifolia* **(Campanulaceae).**

WELTED THISTLE *(Carduus acanthoides)*. This is a
biennial herb of wet hedgerows and waste places. The
erect, winged, cottony stems up to 4 feet high bear
narrow lobed leaves with spiny margins. The heads of
reddish-purple tubular florets appear between June and
August. The one-seeded fruits are crowned with a tuft
of long white pappus hairs **(Compositae).**

WATER THISTLE *(Cirsium oleraceum)*. This is a rare introduced plant, occurring in a few places by streams and in wet woods. It is a perennial herb up to 4 feet high distinguished by its heads of yellowish florets formed from July to September. The **Creeping Thistle** *(C. arvense)* and the **Marsh Thistle** *(C. palustre)* are both very common **(Compositae).**

CARLINE THISTLE *(Carlina vulgaris)* is sometimes common on chalk and limestone grassland. It is a biennial with a tap root, erect stems 4 inches to 2 feet high, and prickly lanceolate leaves. The flowering heads, about 2 inches across, are formed from July until October. The small tubular crimson florets are surrounded by spiny bracts. The one-seeded fruits have tufts of long feathery hairs **(Compositae).**

LESSER KNAPWEED *(Centaurea nigra)*. This is an extremely variable perennial herb, particularly common in grassland. It has narrow lobed leaves and stiff erect stems up to 2 feet high. The solitary heads of tubular florets, surrounded by several rows of brown-fringed bracts, are formed between June and September. The florets are purplish-red or deep purple and sometimes the marginal ones are larger than the others **(Compositae)**.

CORNFLOWER *(Centaurea cyanus)*. This native annual was once a common cornfield weed but has now become rare. Both the stems, which are up to 3 feet high, and the narrow lobed leaves, are covered with cottony hairs. The capitula appear from June until August. The outer blue tubular florets are large and sterile whereas the smaller central reddish-purple ones are hermaphrodite **(Compositae).**

DANDELION *(Taraxacum officinale)*. This well known perennial herb is abundant in pastures, lawns and waste places. It has a strong tap root and a basal rosette of thin, often lobed, leaves. The conspicuous heads of yellow ligulate florets are borne singly on hollow stems between March and October. When mature, the single-seeded fruit bears a parachute of white hairs, which ensure efficient wind dispersal. Although the florets have stamens the pollen is defective and pollination does not occur. However, in spite of this, many viable seeds are formed **(Compositae)**.

MOUSE-EAR HAWKWEED *(Hieracium pilosella)*. This is a small perennial, often found in grassy parts of heaths and pastures. It has a basal rosette of hairy lanceolate leaves and produces creeping rhizomes which form new plantlets. The pale-yellow capitula are borne terminally on erect unbranched stems, 2 to 12 inches high, between May and August. Each of the small florets has a short corolla tube with a flat extension on one side. The one-seeded fruit is black and bears a tuft of long white hairs, which assist in wind dispersal **(Compositae)**.

EDELWEISS *(Leontopodium alpinum)* is an alpine plant, 3 to 6 inches high, occurring in stony limestone pastures. Although not a native it can easily be grown here. The narrow leaves and unbranched stems are covered with woolly hairs. The terminal capitula appear from July to September **(Compositae).**

131

COLTSFOOT *(Tussilago farfara)* is a perennial, commonly found covering large patches of waste and cultivated areas especially on clay soils. It has long white underground rhizomes which give rise to the leaves after the flowers have disappeared. Each leaf has a thick grooved stalk and a rounded blade covered beneath with white woolly hairs. The yellow capitula are borne singly in March and April on slender stems. The outer ray florets are female and the few central disc florets are male. The one-seeded fruit bears a tuft of long white hairs which help in wind dispersal **(Compositae).**

ONE-FLOWERED FLEABANE (*Erigeron uniflorus*). This is a perennial alpine herb which grows in stony ground up to 12,000 feet. It also occurs in Iceland and has been recorded on rocks in the Inner Hebrides. It is 2 to 6 inches tall with a few basal lanceolate leaves. The capitula, which are borne terminally on unbranched stems in July and August, have whitish-purple ray florets and yellow disc florets **(Compositae).**

MOON DAISY (*Chrysanthemum leucanthemum*) is a common grassland herb. It is a perennial with annual stems about 2 feet high. The capitula, which are borne on long stalks from June until August, have large white female ray florets and numerous small bisexual disc florets. The black one-seeded fruits have white ribs **(Compositae)**.

YARROW *(Achillea millefolium)*. This perennial herb is abundant in waste grassland. It has an underground rhizome and erect green stems about 18 inches high with pinnately dissected leaves. The small white crowded capitula appear from June until August. The outer ray florets have no stamens. The small flattened fruits each contain a single seed **(Compositae)**.

WORMWOOD *(Artemesia absinthium)* is a perennial aromatic herb frequent in waste places. The erect ridged stems, up to 3 feet high, and pinnately dissected leaves, are covered with white hairs which give the whole plant a grey-green colour. The small capitula of dull-yellow flowers are formed in July and August. The oil used for flavouring absinthe is extracted from this plant **(Compositae)**.

MUGWORT *(Artemesia vulgaris)* is more common in waste places than the closely related **Wormwood**. It is a larger plant, up to 4 feet high, with leaves which are dark green above and covered with white woolly hairs underneath. The numerous capitula of dull brown florets appear from July to September, and like those of other members of the genus they are wind-pollinated **(Compositae)**.

THE NAMES OF PLANTS

Many of our native plants are known by common names which often refer to some striking feature such as the form of the leaf (Pennywort), the colour and shape of the flower (Snowdrop, Bluebell) or the appearance of the fruit (Storksbill, Old Man's Beard). Yet others refer to their real or supposed medicinal use (Hedge Wound-wort), or to their poisonous nature (Deadly Nightshade). Although these vernacular names are so familiar they are, for a number of reasons, of limited use to the practical botanist who wants to identify and name the plants he finds with precision.

Quite often these common names are misleading; for example, neither Goosegrass nor Cotton Grass is a true grass and the former does not even look like a grass. Further confusion can arise when a plant has several currently-used common names. The Alder Buckthorn is in the same family as the ordinary Buckthorn but it is also known as Black Dogwood, although it is not related to the common Dogwood. There are also regional differences in the use of names; the plant known in Scotland as the Bluebell is called the Harebell in England, where the Bluebell is a very different plant.

In contrast, there are some groups of very similar and closely related plants which are not easily distinguished by the untrained eye, and are in consequence embraced under a single common name (e.g. Common Sedge, Common Rush).

These examples apply only to the limited area of Britain, but the problem is further aggravated in the case of widespread plants which have various common names in different languages.

Another difficulty arises from the fact that generally

only those plants which are conspicuous or are useful or harmful to man have been given common names. This leaves many which have no traditional common names, although it was the habit of some botanists of the last century to invent English names in such cases. This practice was not satisfactory and it is clear that some simple, universal system is required by which all plants can be named without ambiguity.

Gradually a uniform method of plant nomenclature has been built up, and this is governed by universally accepted international rules. In this binomial system each species has a double name, that of the genus to which it belongs followed by the specific epithet. For example, the correct scientific name for Goosegrass is *Galium aparine*, whereas the closely related Lady's Bedstraw is *Galium verum*. In technical publications the scientific name is followed by the name, usually abbreviated, of the author who first correctly described the species. Thus the name of Goosegrass is *Galium aparine* L., the initial standing for Linnaeus, the great eighteenth century Swedish naturalist. There is only one correct scientific name for any particular species, and as this is used throughout the world confusion is greatly reduced.

CLASSIFICATION
OF FLOWERING PLANTS

Fossil evidence indicates that angiosperms were present on this planet at least two hundred million years ago but it is only comparatively recently, in geological terms, that they have become so widespread and abundant. Today they form the dominant and highly diverse vegetation over most of the land surface of the earth. Exact numbers cannot be given, but at least two hundred thousand different kinds or species of flowering plants are known and undoubtedly more remain to be discovered.

Quite apart from the problem of naming and identifying plants, it is clear that some sort of classification of this enormous group is necessary to bring order out of chaos. Linnaeus, in one of the earliest attempts, devised an artificial system based mainly on the numbers of carpels and stamens present in the flower. Although of some use in identifying the limited number of species known at that time, it had the great disadvantage of putting obviously unrelated plants close together. Later so-called natural systems were produced when it was realised that similarities between species implied more or less close relationships.

The general acceptance of the ideas expounded in Darwin's 'Origin of Species', published in 1859, brought about further important changes. If evolution had occurred in the flowering plants, it was necessary for any proposed classification to reflect their past history or *phylogeny*. In other words the uniform flower structure found, for example in the pea family, implies not only that the plants are closely related but also that the group had probably evolved from a common ancestor.

We have seen that closely similar species are put together in genera. These genera are further grouped in families; for example both Lady's Bedstraw (Galium verum) and the Wild Madder (Rubia peregrina) are included in the family Rubiaceae. The exact number of families into which the angiosperms are divided is to some extent a matter of opinion, but there are at least three hundred. They vary in size from those which contain a single unique species to the daisy family (Compositae) with about twenty thousand species.

At the family level floral structures usually provide a more reliable guide to affinity than do the vegetative parts. In the Compositae the inflorescence and floral structure is very uniform and characteristic, while the range of habit is very wide. Further, environmental factors cause far greater variation in the vegetative parts than in the flowers.

John Ray, the 17th century English botanist, was the first to recognise two distinct groups in the flowering plants; the monocotyledons and the dicotyledons. The former, which includes such plants as the lilies, orchids, grasses and sedges, are characterized by a single seed leaf or cotyledon in the embryo. Generally they have narrow leaves with parallel veins, and the floral parts are in threes. On the other hand the dicotyledons have two seed leaves in the embryo, the leaves are often broad and net-veined and the floral parts are generally in fours or fives. This primary division is still valid and indicates that two distinct lines were established at an early stage in the evolution of the angiosperms.

A synopsis of the classification is given on the following three pages in so far as the plants illustrated in this book are concerned. It is generally recognised that the monocotyledons can be divided into three groups; the Calyciferae in which the flowers have a distinct calyx, the Corolliferae with a colourful perianth of two similar whorls, and the Glumiflorae which have small flowers with the perianth reduced or absent. The primary division of the dicotyledons is into the Archichlamydeae, where the petals are free, and the Metachlamydeae, which have the petals more or less fused together. This division is rather a matter of convenience and some botanists do not accept it as a natural one. More likely the sympetalous families have evolved along a number of distinct lines from different polypetalous types.

It will be noticed that the families are grouped under orders which represent wider spheres of affinity. Until more is known about the past history of the angiosperms the relationship of these orders to one another is largely a matter of opinion, and no evolutionary significance should be attached to their position in the lists.

MONOCOTYLEDONES

CALYCIFERAE
   ALISMATALES
      Alismataceae - Water Plantain, Arrowhead
      Butomaceae - Flowering Rush
   NAJADALES
      Potamogetonaceae - Pondweed
COROLLIFERAE
   LILIALES
      Liliaceae - Bluebell, Autumn Crocus
      Trilliaceae - Herb Paris
   AMARYLLIDALES
      Amaryllidaceae - Daffodil, Snowdrop
   ORCHIDALES
      Orchidaceae - Spotted Orchid, Fly Orchid
   TYPHALES
      Typhaceae - Reedmace
      Sparganiaceae - Bur-reed
GLUMIFLORAE
   CYPERALES
      Cyperaceae - Bulrush, Cotton Grass
   GRAMINALES
      Gramineae - Sweet Vernal Grass, Meadow Grass

DICOTYLEDONES-ARCHICHLAMYDEAE

RANALES
  Ranunculaceae - Stinking Hellebore, Goldilocks
  Berberidaceae - Barberry
RHOEDALES
  Papaveraceae - Field Poppy
  Fumariaceae - Common Fumitory
  Cruciferae - Wallflower, Lady's Smock
  Resedaceae - Dyer's Rocket
VIOLALES
  Violaceae - Sweet Violet
BIXALES
  Cistaceae - Common Rockrose
CARYOPHYLLALES
  Caryophyllaceae - Ragged Robin
  Portulacaceae - Sun Plant
MALVALES
  Malvaceae - Common Mallow
GERANIALES
  Geraniaceae - Common Storksbill
  Oxalidaceae - Wood Sorrel
RHAMNALES
  Rhamnaceae - Alder Buckthorn
LEGUMINOSAE
  Papilionaceae - Birdsfoot, Clovers
ROSALES
  Rosaceae - Dog Rose, Wild Strawberry
  Saxifragaceae - Meadow Saxifrage
MYRTALES
  Lythraceae - Purple Loosestrife
  Onagraceae - Rosebay Willow-herb, Evening Primrose
UMBELLALES
  Umbelliferae - Wild Carrot, Fool's Parsley
  Araliaceae - Ivy
CUCURBITALES
  Cucurbitaceae - White Bryony
ARISTOLOCHIACEAE
  Aristolochiaceae - Birthwort
EUPHORBIALES
  Euphorbiaceae - Sun Spurge

DICOTYLEDONES-METACHLAMYDEAE

ERICALES
  Ericaceae - Ling, Bilberry
PLUMBAGINALES
  Plumbaginaceae - Thrift
PRIMULALES
  Primulaceae - Cowslip, Scarlet Pimpernel
GENTIANALES
  Gentianaceae - Gentian
  Menyanthaceae - Bogbean
APOCYNALES
  Apocynaceae - Lesser Periwinkle
SOLANALES
  Solanaceae - Thorn Apple, Deadly Nightshade
  Convolvulaceae - Bindweed, Dodder
PERSONALES
  Scrophulariaceae - Figwort, Foxglove, Toadflax
  Orobanchaceae - Broomrape
BORAGINALES
  Boraginaceae - Viper's Bugloss, Forget-me-not
LAMIALES
  Labiatae - Red Deadnettle, Bugle
RUBIALES
  Rubiaceae - Goosegrass, Lady's Bedstraw
  Caprifoliaceae - Elder, Honeysuckle
VALERIANALES
  Valerianaceae - Valerian
  Dipsacaceae - Field Scabious, Teasel
CAMPANULALES
  Campanulaceae - Clustered Bellflower, Rampion
ASTERALES
  Compositae - Dandelion, Moon Daisy, Wormwood

GLOSSARY OF BOTANICAL TERMS

Achene: a small, dry, indehiscent fruit, formed from a single carpel, which contains a single seed.

Actinomorphic: a flower which has more than one vertical plane of symmetry, e.g. Cowslip.

Alternate: leaves inserted at different levels along a stem.

Androecium: the male part of the flower, composed of one or more stamens.

Anther: the swollen terminal part of a stamen, containing the pollen.

Apetalous: a flower without petals.

Apocarpous: a gynoecium in which the carpels are not fused to one another, i.e. free.

Axillary: a bud or flower borne in an axil; that is, the upper angle formed between the stem and an attached leaf.

Berry: a fleshy fruit which contains several seeds.

Bract: a small leaf borne on a stem, often subtending a flower.

Bulb: an underground perennating structure with a short stem and swollen leaves or leaf bases containing stored food material.

Bulbil: a small swollen structure in the axil of a leaf which becomes detached as an organ of vegetative reproduction.

Calyx: the outer perianth whorl of the flower, the sepals.

Capitulum: a compact inflorescence of numerous small flowers borne on a flat or convex receptacle, e.g. Dandelion.

Capsule: a dry dehiscent fruit which opens by pores or valves to release the seeds.

Carpel: one of the units of the female part of the flower which produces ovules.

Cladode: a flattened leaf-like stem, e.g. Butcher's Broom.

Corm: an underground perennating structure consisting of a short vertical stem swollen with food reserves.

Corolla: the inner perianth whorl of the flower, the petals.

Corymb: a crowded inflorescence with the pedicels of different lengths so that the flowers are all at the same level.

Cotyledon: the first one or two leaves of an embryo present in the seed. They may be thick or thin and may either remain below ground or become exposed when the seed germinates.

Cyme: an inflorescence in which the apex is terminated by a flower so that further flowers are formed from laterals below.

Dioecious: a species in which male and female flowers are borne on separate plants.

Disc-floret: the small, central tubular flowers often present in a capitulum, e.g. Coltsfoot.

Drupe: a fleshy indehiscent fruit, with the innermost part of the ovary wall forming a stony layer around the one or few seeds.

Epipetalous: stamens borne on the petals or corolla tube.

Filament: the slender unbranched stalk of a stamen which bears the anther.

Floret: a small flower, usually applied to those in the crowded inflorescences of the Compositae and Gramineae.

Follicle: a dry dehiscent fruit, formed from a single carpel, containing several seeds which are shed by a split along one side of the wall.

Fruit: the structure containing the seeds formed after fertilisation.

Gamopetalous: a corolla with the petals partially or completely fused together.

Gynoecium: the female part of the flower composed of one or more carpels.

Hermaphrodite: a flower with both male and female organs.

Inferior: an ovary sunk into and fused with the deep concave receptacle so that the other floral parts are borne above it.

Inflorescence: a group of flowers, including the stems on which they are borne.

Internode: a portion of a stem between the insertion of two successive leaves.

Involucre: a group of bracts surrounding a capitulum.

Lamina: the flattened blade of a leaf.

Monoecious: with separate male and female flowers borne on the same plant.

Nectary: a part of the flower which produces nectar, often on a petal or the receptacle.

Node: a region of a stem where a leaf is attached.

Nut: a single-seeded fruit with a hard woody wall.

Nutlet: a small indehiscent portion of a fruit containing a single seed, e.g. Labiatae.

Opposite: where two leaves are inserted on either side of the same node.

Ovary: the hollow basal part of a carpel, containing one or more ovules.

Ovule: a structure within the ovary which becomes a seed after fertilisation.

Palmate: a compound leaf with the leaflets attached to the end of the petiole.

Panicle: a branched racemose inflorescence.

Pedicel: a stalk of a single flower.

Peduncle: the stalk of a whole inflorescence.

Perianth: the outer floral parts; they may all be alike or distinguished into sepals and petals.

Petal: one of the members of the inner perianth whorl, often brightly coloured.

Petiole: a leaf stalk.

Pinnate: a compound leaf with the leaflets arranged in two lateral rows.

Pod: a dry dehiscent fruit, formed from a single carpel, containing one or several seeds which are released when the ovary wall splits along the edges.

Pollen: microscopic grains produced in the anthers which are transferred to the stigma. Here they germinate and produce a tube which grows down the style and enters an ovule where it effects fertilisation.

Polypetalous: a corolla with the petals not fused to one another, i.e. free.

Raceme: an inflorescence in which the growing point does not give rise to a flower. The stalked flowers are borne laterally on the main axis with the oldest at the base.

Radical: leaves which arise at ground level, often forming a basal rosette.

Ray-floret: the small outer flowers of a capitulum, with strap-shaped corollas.

Receptacle: the central axis of the flower to which the floral parts are attached. It may be concave, flat or convex. Also used for the disc which bears the florets of a capitulum.

Rhizome: a horizontal perennating underground stem.

Seed: the reproductive structure formed from an ovule after fertilisation. It contains an embryo and food store and is covered by the seed coat or testa.

Sepal: one of the members of the outer perianth whorl, often green and protecting the other parts of the flower-bud.

Sessile: without a stalk.

Siliqua: a long, narrow, dehiscent fruit found in the cress family. It usually opens from below upwards by two valves.

Spike: a raceme with sessile flowers.

Spikelet: the inflorescence unit in the grass family. It consists of one or more minute florets enclosed by sterile bracts.

151

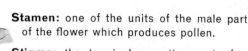

Stamen: one of the units of the male part of the flower which produces pollen.

Stigma: the terminal receptive part of a carpel on which the pollen grains germinate.

Style: a part of the carpel which bears the stigma and down which the pollen tube grows towards the ovary.

Superior: an ovary with the other floral parts inserted below it.

Sympetalous: a corolla with the petals partially or completely fused together.

Synocarpous: a gynoecium with the carpels joined together. Fusion may involve only the ovaries (Ragged Robin), the ovaries and styles (Mallow), or the ovaries, styles and stigmas (Cowslip).

Tendril: a coiled climbing organ which may be the whole or part of a stem or leaf.

Terminal: a flower borne at the end of a stem and thus preventing any further growth.

Tuber: an underground perennating structure which only exists for a year. It may be a swollen region of a stem or root.

Umbel: an inflorescence in which all the pedicels arise from one point at the end of the peduncle. It may be simple or compound.

Zygomorphic: a flower with only one plane of symmetry, e.g. Foxglove.

BIBLIOGRAPHY

Clapham, A. R., Tutin, T. G. & Warburg, E. F. **Flora of the British Isles** (2nd ed.). Cambridge University Press, 1962.

Gilmour, J. & Walters, M. **Wild Flowers.** Collins, New Naturalist, No. 5, 1954.

Hubbard, C. E. **Grasses.** Penguin Books Ltd., 1954.

Hutchinson, J. **British Wild Flowers,** Vols. I & II. Penguin Books Ltd., 1955.

Lewis, P. **British Wild Flowers.** Eyre & Spottiswoode, 1958.

McLintock, D. & Fitter, R. S. R. **The Pocket Guide to Wild Flowers.** Collins, 1956.

Salisbury, E. **Weeds and Aliens.** Collins, New Naturalist, No. 43, 1961.

Turrill, W. B. **British Plant Life.** Collins, New Naturalist, No. 10, 1948.

INDEX